Curious George DISCOVERS the Stars

Adaptation by Bethany V. Freitas

Based on the TV series teleplay
written by Raye Lankford

Houghton Mifflin Harcourt
Boston   New York

Photo credits:

Photograph on cover (left) courtesy of NASA

Photographs on cover (right) and pp. 4, 13, 15, and 17 courtesy of Houghton Mifflin Harcourt

Photographs on pp. 11, 31 (right), and 32 courtesy of HMH/Carrie Garcia

Photographs on pp. 22 and 26 courtesy of Dave Curtin

Photograph on page 31 (background) courtesy of Jon Whittle

For information about permission to reproduce selections from this book, write to Permissions, Houghton Mifflin Harcourt Publishing Company, 215 Park Avenue South, New York, New York 10003.

ISBN: 978-0-544-65162-3 paper over board

ISBN: 978-0-544-65164-7 paperback

Art adaptation by Rudy Obrero and Kaci Obrero

Design by Susanna Vagt

www.hmhco.com

Printed in China

SCP 10 9 8 7 6 5 4 3 2 1

4500579127

Have you ever wondered how many stars there are in the sky? George has—especially when he's in the country. In the country, the summer nights are cool, you can hear frogs croaking, and the sky is full of stars.

One night, George was outside looking at the sky when he heard Bill's voice.

"Hi, George! It's a great night for stargazing," Bill called from his window. But George wasn't just looking at the stars. He was trying to figure out how many stars there were in the sky—there must be hundreds! "Not even scientists know how many stars are up there," Bill said.

George thought it was time somebody found out!

Did you know . . .

scientists who study stars are called astronomers? People have looked at the stars and wondered about the mysteries of space for thousands of years. Early astronomers used the stars in the sky to find their way and to make calendars. We still use some of their methods today.

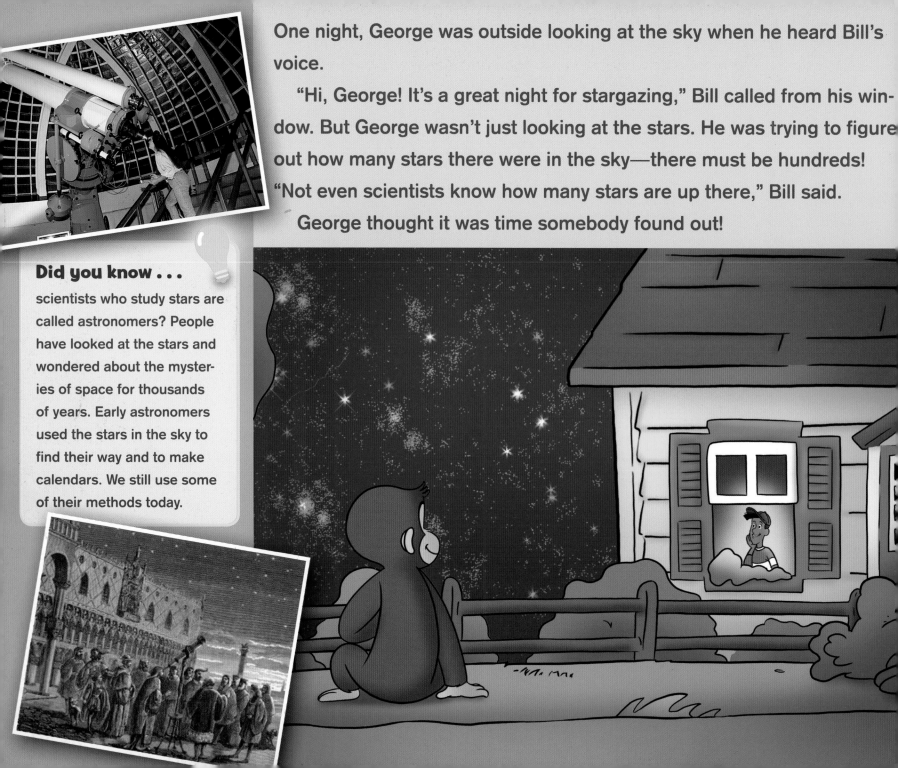

George knew the most important rule of counting anything was keeping track. He found a notepad and pencil and made a mark for each star as he counted it. There were so many stars to keep track of, but he kept at it: One, two, three, four, five . . .

But George fell asleep midcount! That was okay. After a good night's rest he would be ready to start counting again the next night.

There was only one problem: His counting system didn't keep track of which stars he had already counted. So last night's count didn't count! George figured the only way he could count the stars without losing track was to count all the stars really fast before he fell asleep.

But George wasn't fast enough.

Bill stopped by the following day. "Morning, fellas!"

The man waved, but George still felt sleepy. "George was up late counting stars," the man said.

"Too bad you can't count stars during the day. They are always up there, you know," Bill said. "We just can't see them because the sun is so bright."

George wasn't so sure. He wondered what really happened to stars during the day. Maybe they went to sleep, or got blown out like candles on a birthday cake. Wherever they went, George couldn't count stars he couldn't see.

"There are lots of differences between the sky during the day and the sky at night," the man said. "We can see the moon and the stars at night, but we can see the sun only during the day."

"Right!" said Bill. "Because at night, the sun is shining on the other side of Earth. When it's nighttime here, it's daytime there!"

When it came to day sky and night sky, George was sure about two things: he couldn't count stars during the day, and he couldn't count all of the stars in one night. But he wasn't going to give up.

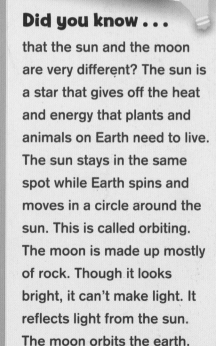

Did you know . . .

that the sun and the moon are very different? The sun is a star that gives off the heat and energy that plants and animals on Earth need to live. The sun stays in the same spot while Earth spins and moves in a circle around the sun. This is called orbiting. The moon is made up mostly of rock. Though it looks bright, it can't make light. It reflects light from the sun. The moon orbits the earth.

George took a good long look at the night sky. The stars were scattered around like confetti. And, like with confetti, there wasn't a pattern to the way they were arranged. Unless . . .

George noticed a group of stars that looked familiar. They looked like a big upside-down cap!

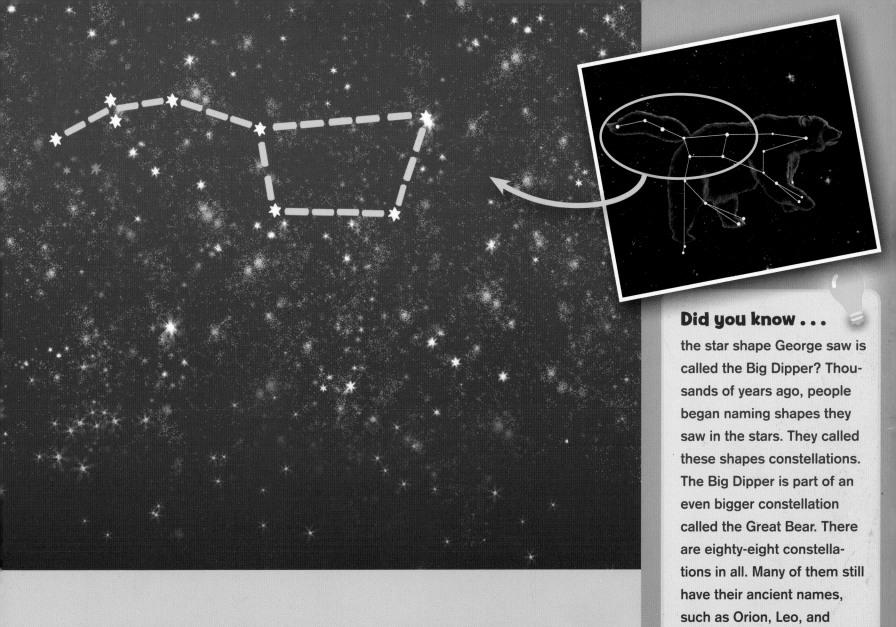

Did you know . . .

the star shape George saw is called the Big Dipper? Thousands of years ago, people began naming shapes they saw in the stars. They called these shapes constellations. The Big Dipper is part of an even bigger constellation called the Great Bear. There are eighty-eight constellations in all. Many of them still have their ancient names, such as Orion, Leo, and Scorpio. These star shapes were named by astronomers and used to map the sky, just like George did.

George could use this star shape as a place keeper. He counted the stars below it and marked them on his pad. Then he counted the stars above it and on each side.

George had a system! He could use star shapes to keep track of which stars he had already counted. When he got tired, he could go to bed and know where he left off for the next night's count.

At the end of the week, it was time for George and the man to return to the city. George had made a lot of progress on his star-counting. And now that he had a system, he could count stars in the city, too. "Big, hot city, here we come!" the man said.

The city was very hot. George couldn't wait to get into the cool, air-conditioned lobby.

But it was just as warm inside their building as it was outside.

"Is the air conditioner broken?" the man asked.

"No," said the doorman. "But we're not allowed to use it. You'll have to keep yours off in your apartment, too."

George wondered why. "Too many air conditioners running at once uses a lot of electricity. It can cause the power to go out," the man said. "I guess we'll be a little warm tonight."

But George wasn't worried about electricity and being too hot. He had stars to count!

George knew he would have a great view of the sky from the roof. But when he got up there and looked around, he noticed something strange. In the city, he couldn't see any stars at all!

George went back to the apartment to see his friend. "It's tough to count stars in the big, bright city," the man explained. George was confused. "It's like trying to count stars during the daytime. They're up there, but we can't see them."

With no stars to count, George figured he might as well go to bed. But it was too hot to sleep. The one time he could have stayed awake all night long to count, he couldn't see a single star!

George took a walk out onto the balcony. His neighbors had their air conditioners on. George could hear them humming. Would it really hurt if he turned their AC on? Just for a minute?

The cold air felt good on George's face. But a moment later, the AC—and all of the lights in the apartment—went out!

Did you know . . .

that "blackout" is another word for a power outage? A blackout can happen for a lot of reasons. Windy weather and falling trees can damage power lines, for example. And if too many people in one area use a lot of electricity at the same time, the system might shut down. Important buildings like hospitals have backup generators that can give them power during a blackout.

George ran back up to the roof. Uh-oh. The lights were out in all the buildings around them. Could one curious little monkey cause a citywide blackout? George didn't know, but there was only one thing to do at a time like this—hide!

Before long the man found George in his hiding spot. George was upset about turning off the city's electricity. "It wasn't your fault, George!" the man said. "It takes more than one little monkey to cause a blackout."

Just then the doorman and Hundley joined them on the roof.
"This blackout's really something, isn't it?" the doorman asked.
"Yes," said the man. "But George thinks the blackout was his fault. He turned on our air conditioner."

"I thought it was my fault too!" said the doorman. "Hundley was so hot, I turned on our AC for just a minute. Then all the lights went out. I bet a lot people thought the same thing." George was relieved!

"Well, George, there is one good thing about this blackout. Now you can see the stars!" It was true! Now that all of the electrical lights were out and the city was dark, he could see the sky full of stars again. George found the Big Upside-Down Cap and settled in for a good, long star-count.

Make Your Own Constellations Viewer

The Big Upside-Down Cap—better known as the Big Dipper—is one of many constellations that are visible in the night sky. Learn the names and shapes of a few famous constellations by making your own constellations viewer!

You will need . . .

- empty toilet paper or paper towel tubes
- tinfoil
- notebook paper or tracing paper
- tape
- scissors
- a sharp pencil, safety pin, or thumbtack
- scrap cardboard or cork board
- rubber bands

What to do:

1. Pick a constellation to view! Lay your notebook paper or tracing paper over one of the constellations on the next page and trace the template for your constellation.

2. Cut a circle around your template with your scissors and set it aside.

3. Cut a piece of tinfoil big enough to cover the end of your tube. A 4 x 4 inch square should do it.

4. Tape your constellation template to the center of the piece of tinfoil.

5. Place the foil and template on top of your cardboard or cork. Use the sharp pencil, pin, or thumbtack to poke a small hole in each dot on the template.

6. Place the foil over the end of your tube, template side in. Make sure it's centered so all of the holes are over the opening. Gently fold the extra foil around the tube and use a rubber band to hold it in place.

7. You can use markers or paint to decorate your tube. You may also want to write the name of the constellation on the side.

8. Close one eye and look through the open end of your tube with the other. Do you see your constellation? Now you can look at the stars inside, during the day, anytime! Make a few different constellation viewers and quiz your friends on which constel- lation is which.

Constellations don't just have names—they have stories, too! Learn more about some famous constellations and be sure to look for them next time you're under a starry sky:

Ursa Major, the Great Bear

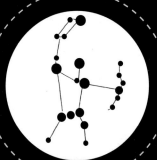

Ursa Major was first spotted in the sky and named almost two thousand years ago. Many different civilizations told stories about the big bear in the sky. Do you see the Big Dipper?

Orion, the Hunter

Not all constellations are animals. Orion was named after an ancient Greek warrior. He is easy to spot by the three bright stars that make up his belt.

Leo, the Lion

Leo was another of the first constellations to be named, and is one of the easiest to see thanks to his crouching-lion shape. You could say Leo is king of the jungle and king of the sky!

Canis Major, the Big Dog

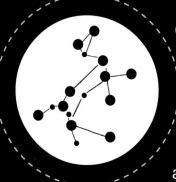

You can find Big Dog by looking for his tag: Sirius, one of the closest stars to Earth. Even if Big Dog runs away, you'll always be able to find him with the help of Sirius!